My Life as a
Thought…

A Journey of Grace, Growth & God

TONY ROUSE

MY LIFE AS A THOUGHT...

ISBN: 0692672311
ISBN-13: 978-0692672310

DEDICATION

This book is dedicated to you... The Reader. It is my sincere hope that you reflect upon your own life as you read through the thoughts from mine. Thank you for reading.

MY LIFE AS A THOUGHT…

CONTENTS

MY LIFE AS A THOUGHT...

ACKNOWLEDGMENTS

I'd like to acknowledge my family, who have always been there for me with voluntary and involuntary support… I'd like to thank all of my friends for a continuous understanding of 'My Next Great Idea'. And lastly, I appreciate all of my mentors for talking me off the ledge when I needed it and at times pushing me over it because I wouldn't have gone otherwise…

Thank You:

Minister Donna Alexander
Mr. & Mrs. LeeMoyne & Brenda Canady
Mr. & Mrs. Wes & Bernadine Cantrell
Mr. & Mrs. Terence & Constance Caston
Pastors Creflo & Taffi Dollar
Pastors Craig & Natarsha Garcia
Mr. & Mrs. Lewis & Gwen Rouse
Mr. & Mrs. Mike & Jean Roussell
Pastors Kyle & Tina Self
Mr. Harry Webber

MY LIFE AS A THOUGHT...

1: INTRODUCTION

For such a time as this...

Greetings! My name is Tony Rouse and I am very excited that you have decided to 'hitch a ride' on this journey through the recesses of my mind. It is my hope that this experience is as awesome for you as it was for me (in retrospect that is...).

My Life as a Thought... is literally just that. This book is a collection of observances, thoughts, hopes, visions and dreams that I've experienced over the past few years making my way through this thing we all call life. It explores the conversations of encouragement and moments of enlightenment that I have had to have with myself while in the same thought, seemingly addressing a multitude of people simultaneously. Excerpts are taken from my various platforms on social media and things found in my personal journal, what I refer to as: 'The Life of Tony Rouse'.

We begin in February of 2016 and proceed in reverse chronological order throughout time and explore topics that are honest, funny, familiar, poignant and relevant. I'll be the first to say that this book is not a shrine unto myself, but rather it is a reflective moment of things to think about as you go through your own everyday challenges of life. It is meant to build up your strengths and breakdown your weaknesses and to ultimately have 'Real Talk' with the 'Real You'.

I'll be the first to tell you... Life has kicked me in the mouth. But the thing is... even when I wanted to... I didn't quit. What I've learned along the way was how to stay positive in spite of all the craziness that was around me. What I came to realize more than anything else was that I was in control of my life and had to take back everything that was taken from me.

The most pivotal point of transformation for me came when I realized that I had something to be truly thankful for. Whether it was the breath in my lungs or the sunshine on my face... I was determined to be thankful. I believe far too often, many get in a sense of comparison with others instead of just being grateful for the very gifts that they do have.

The subtitle to this book states: 'A Journey of Grace,

Growth & God' and that is exactly what my life has been. It's evident Grace is present simply because I have personally been equipped with so much that is meant to share with so many.... but here's the kicker... you need to know that YOU have so much to share with others as well. My Growth came from the fact that I let fear operate for far too long for much of my life. I would always push and encourage others, but I wasn't pushing myself as hard as could have, but when I finally decided to flip from fear to faith... it was on and poppin' (this is a hip-hop reference for those that don't know...). In all honesty, this book probably could have been written 5 years ago, but then when you apply the God factor... it all has to be completed in His perfect timing and now I'm in a position and place where I understand my mission, I recognize my calling and I'm willing to accept the challenge of fighting through, fighting on and winning in life and showing people what it takes to conquer those situations and issues that may seem impossible and insurmountable, but are really only light weight workouts of your faith.

I'll say this... this is not some cheap and cheesy Christian manual for life or anything close to it. There are scripture references contained and yes I will say Jesus, God, etc., but the big picture is that I want you to see that I can only speak from the experiences that I've had and know. For me, authenticity is one of the most important character traits to possess only because it's the real you that no one knows, but should. I think that we have to be honest with ourselves and be willing to share our experiences because (here's some insight into truth…) the things that you went through were not for you… They are actually situations used to help you build up others.

Last but not least, I want you to understand that this book is straight and to the point. The entries are not filled with fluff because I don't think in fluff. As a heads up, there are some times throughout the years listed that have no entry simply because at that time, I had nothing to say (I'm referencing '08 and '09). With all that being said… Thank You for this experience.

Enjoy the Ride.
Tony Rouse

2: TWO THOUSAND SIXTEEN
"The Year of The Restart"

February 29 · Stop posting your private actions in public places. Every move isn't meant to be seen.

February 23 · You can never be ahead of your time. Someone has to be a revolutionary to change the way others think... Even if they do finally catch up 5-20 years later.

February 23 · Time is going to pass whether you take advantage of it or not. What I'm starting to realize is that many of us make a lot of noise, but not a lot of moves.

February 20 · I believe that far too often we abandon our dreams. We treat them as if they are a 'nice to have' opportunity as opposed to the life-fulfilling calling that they are truly meant to be. These grand ideas don't just show up in your life as 'that'll never be me' moments, but rather they are revealed to you because in a sense it is your true identity to make these things happen and be brought to life.

February 18 · I believe this election is being driven by who people will not vote for as opposed to who they actually support. And this is on both sides...

February 18 · Don't get stuck or quit while in your process. I woke up this morning thinking about Daniel in the lion's den. What looked like sure death was only a time used to represent true grace. Daniel decided not to abandon his faith when it all looked crazy and the result was that he showed an entire nation what it meant to believe God in spite of what it may cost. So many times we give up when things 'seem' to not be going our way, but in reality if we just stand in faith, trust and believe that all things are working for our good... We shall surely see the goodness of the Lord in the land of the living.

February 17 · I've got the Power.

February 17 · Breakthrough: The pivotal point in an altercation when all things shift and turn in your favor.

February 15 · I don't live my life to adapt. I live to be adept.

February 15 · Don't speak against those things of which you know not of...

February 15 · You have to know when people are in it with you and when they are in it for themselves. Loyalty is a commodity that everyone isn't willing to pay for.

February 15 · For so long I was always in a rush for the wrong things. The problem with that is that you are chasing things that should be chasing you...

February 15 · When it's free... Ask questions. Many times there is a reason why there is no value associated with a particular item.

February 14 · It is my job to speak life into others peoples' lives. At my last stop, I was at a table with a couple that's been married for nine years and in their words you could hear the frustration of things that were going wrong in their life. They even brought up that the past two years have been some crazy things as well. What was so dope is that even in that place... I just reminded them of how God loved them first (1 John 4:19) and how they could trust that, depend on it and lean on it. What was funny was that the guy just asked "Can I hug you? Like hug you with a with a real hug?" (For those that don't know... I'm not into invasion of personal space without the required handshake, but this time

I was like it's cool...) I tell you this in that moment you could feel the lifting of a weight and almost a renewed sense of "Thank You. I'm Going to Make It." #MissionJesus #CauseEffect

February 10 · You have to be wise enough to recognize when people are begging for attention and in that same moment know that the best remedy for this behavior is not to give it to them.

February 10 · Ash Wednesday is an observance of Lent. Ashy on Wednesday is neglected used of Queen Helene's Cocoa Butter.

February 10 · Many times you won't be thanked for all the work that you've done and at some point that has to be okay.

February 8 · Always remain teachable and be easy to correct course. The more you step out and move beyond your comfort zone you may make a mistake, but it is better to gain insight and understanding from being willing to assist than to become stale and stagnant from a lack of association.

February 8 · Here's the thing about social media and the Internet... It costs nothing to post an opinion and because it's free, everyone gets in on it.

February 7 · I honestly believe we all have the capacity to do more. To be honest, I'm not as busy as I think I am. It's all about time prioritization. So make more time for your family. Make more time for your friends. Make more time for causes you care about. Make more time for you.

February 4 · You don't have to be super deep to be effective. Remember: Smile and tell yourself, 'I matter just because God loves me.'

February 4 · Depression and suicide is real, but it's not greater than Jesus.

February 4 · People will actually pay you more money for you to tell them how to do something than they do if you actually do it for them.

February 3 · How many people are thankful in spite of?!? I think if we all took the time... we could easily have a laundry list of problems, but what if we took that same amount of time to focus on the things we are just thankful for in spite of. When we shift our focus of 'what we see', we then expand the capacity of 'how we see'.

February 3 · Faith is not just a movement of your mouth... it is also belief with your heart. The interesting thing about a belief in your heart is that it will cause action in your life. Belief in something will move you further than you've ever imagined simply because in your mind, thought and life you already know it to be true. You simply are waiting for everybody else to catch up...

February 3 · The difference between the Tony Rouse of today vs. the Tony Rouse of yesterday is Precision. There is something about time spent honing your craft and perfecting execution.

February 2 · Just because someone is gifted... Doesn't mean that you're not. If you would spend more time focusing on your unique greatness and not coveting the gifts and talents of others... You'll have more time and opportunity to celebrate the awesomeness of your very own life.

February 2 · People want to put you in a box because that is their most comfortable place to categorize you. Let me make this public service announcement... That "box" is just like a coffin... The only thing that resides there are dead things and people. Rise up and take back your life. Realize that you have been set free to experience this life in all manner of great grace. Take back your dreams. Take back your joy. Take back your peace. If you didn't have a purpose and plan left for your life you wouldn't be here reading this right now. This ain't about hype, this is how you experience a life filled with hope.

February 1 · When I could've quit... I didn't. When it got tough... I endured. When everything looked crazy... I held on. And for that alone... I know God loves me.

January 29 · Just stay faithful.

January 19 · Build. Your. Own.

January 18 · You don't have to ask permission from anyone to be great. It is not my job to make you like/accept/be with me. Far too often we do anything to get in and then you realize... you can't get out.

January 16 · Know your real enemy. "For we wrestle not against flesh and blood..."

January 16 · Think about your life in terms of Social Media... Just because they didn't 'Like' your status, doesn't mean you didn't make an impression.

January 16 · I want my MTV... Money, Time and Value. If you can either save money and/or make time as it relates to other people... You will exponentially increase your value!

January 11 · I grew tired of the world telling me 'No.'... so I told myself 'Yes.'

January 9 · If anyone in business or in life ever tells you that they achieved a significant level of success on their own... Look them square in the face and ask: Why You Always Lying?!?

January 5 · People see you as they see themselves... Many times we get offended with the way people treat us or are bothered by the things that they say about us that may be untrue and we take it personal when many times it honestly has nothing to do with us. Don't let the opinions and thoughts from other people attempt to block your ability to shine. At the end of the day their saltiness ain't got nothing to do with you.

January 4 · Principles don't change... People do.

January 4 · I believe one of the major dangers we all are facing right now is that people have become vigilantes and find themselves lost with no foundation. Thoughts, feelings and action of change are wonderful, but if they are present without an intended direction and/or destination... the results and structure you find are in a sense of chaos and confusion.

3: TWO THOUSAND FIFTEEN
"The Year of The Rebirth"

December 31 · I'm kinda over this New Year's hype already. I think what we've lost is that things don't fall out of the sky into our lap, but rather we speak them into existence. I know it sounds crazy and brutally honest, but the reason why you are exactly where you are is because you've believed it, willed it and spoke it into existence. It is true where you change your thinking you change your life, but don't forget that with that you also have to change what you say. Your mouth has either gotten you into more trouble or brought you more success than anything you've ever dealt with. Get your mouth and mind... and you'll get your life.

December 26 · Time as it depends on months is man made to dictate a cycle. It's not the fact that January 1 signifies the repeat of a cycle, but rather the completion of a season. I find it interesting that New Year's starts in the season of winter when typically everything lies dormant and preparation of opening up in the spring. So often we expect January 1 and/or 2nd to automatically signify a complete change where we've been fully developed like abracadabra when in reality... just like in nature you have to understand you have to come out of winter and move into spring. Change is not an overnight process, but you will never be changed unless you start.

December 22 · Many times the only thing you have left to hold on to is your dream.

December 17 · A soft answer turneth away wrath; but grievous words stir up anger. *Explanation:* So the next time you just got to 'keep it real'... don't be surprised when someone gets 'realer' than you with you. (Tony Rouse Remix of Proverbs 15:1)

December 15 · Airplanes don't argue with rowboats.

December 15 · "To all the ladies in the place with style and grace..." (Artist: Notorious B.I.G. – Song: Big Poppa) *Interpretation:* Even Biggie knew that Grace was important! You see that he took the time to address 'these' ladies directly... He didn't say to all the ladies up in here... Just anybody. No. He specifically said "...with Style and Grace." Now I can't co-sign everything else, but this part reigns true to this day. Hip-Hop will preach if you let it...

December 15 · The greatest need facing today's generation is a complete sense and understanding of their identity. When you recognize who and whose you are... you realize that it changes everything that you do. Your responses to life challenges are just different and now you just know that everything is going to be okay. In a sense you go from panic to planted... From worry and doubt to He'll bring me out.

December 14 · There is a difference between Care and Compromise...

December 14 · We 'gon be alright...

December 14 · Who I am and what I do are two completely different things. What I do as an occupation does not define me, but rather it simply is the expression of my identity already founded in Grace. So many times kids get asked the question, "What do you want to BE when you grow up?" Then answers are encouraged and range from doctor, lawyer, etc. But the reality is that those are merely occupations... not an identity. The identity of who we all should be is love. Especially from a Christian perspective... if people don't see Jesus when they see you, you have to get real with yourself and evaluate your life choices and actions towards yourself and other people. It's easy to say what you do from a digital platform, but when you check back into your real life and the real world and not a fake and phony propagated reality of a digital domain you've created... what is really said then?!? Have you been light? Have you been love? Have you been Grace? And if the answer is yes then great, but don't celebrate the 'Have Been' status of a 'Has Been". Every day we have an opportunity to make and create an impact for a better tomorrow for ourselves and for others.

December 11 · Struggle is not the only the form of evaluation. Yes, it's great to know that people will roll with you when you don't have, but will they want to associate with you when you do. *Meaning:* Everyone can't handle next-level success simply because they don't know how to treat people.

December 10 · How awesome is it to step into someone's life and create an unexpected encounter with favor?

December 10 · "No one on the corner has swagger like Tone... Swagger like Tone. Swagger...Swagger like Tone. No one on the corner... Mr. Rouse is in the Building. My swagger on a hundred, thousand trillion..." Yeah... it's not uncommon for me to remix a rap song with my own name. I figure if I'm going to shout something out I might as well make it apply to my own life...

December 10 · This is a great reminder for those that feel they are behind in life. *Remember:* Don't compare yourself to anyone else's journey... Run the race you've been given. There are great and amazing things planned for your life that you have no clue about, but if you keep looking over at someone else's lane... you can't stay in your own. Believe that God loves you. Receive the fact that you are special and constantly on His mind. Then finally... Achieve your wildest dreams.

December 9 · You have to move with clarity. I'm also thankful for the ability to ask questions and get definitive answers.

December 9 · That moment when you speak truth even when it's uncomfortable...

December 8 · Beloved = "Be Loved." So many people are searching for love externally, but have no real understanding that this is an internal process first. Love is a gift that was already freely given and all you have to do is willingly accept it (John 3:16) But on the flip side... Ask yourself a question... "How Can I 'Be Love'?" People need you and you know it. Don't sit back and wait for them to ask you for help so you can feel that you have power... Help them because you can and know that they need it. Personally, I have an identity of love and recently it has grown to be much stronger than I ever imagined. So I challenge all of my friends this season... whether you need to "Be Loved" and accept it or "Be Love" and present it. We were built to Love. It is truly the most powerful force on this planet, but the problem has been we never fully accepted the true and full identity of it. #TheGiftOfLove

December 8 · Though thy beginning was small...

December 4 · Don't look at where I am... Pay attention to where I'm going.

December 3 · Fear & Laziness will forever keep you out of the Promises of God.

December 2 · In dealing with people in Relationships whether it be Romantic, Business or Personal… Ask yourself one question: "Do they Complement or Complicate?!?"

December 2 · Get to the point to where you celebrate other people more than you celebrate yourself.

December 2 · I know who I am. I know what I've been called to do. I will change the world. I am a World Changer.

November 30 · It only takes one seed to grow an entire tree. Your words and thoughts are just like those seeds... The forest you now have is called your life... Don't like it?!? Change what you are planting.

November 24 · One of my first self-created jobs was personal brand-building for guys. Basically I helped some dudes out very similar to Will Smith in Hitch. And so yesterday I received a Save the Date from one of them that thought he'd never have a girlfriend, let alone be ready to marry the woman of his dreams that loves him for exactly who he is. I knew he was a great dude the entire time, but he didn't see it then. I say all of that to say... Many times we don't or can't see what is truly in us because we have spent so much time comparing ourselves to other people and not valuing the gifts that we've been given. So I encourage you... Spend time with yourself. Be your own best friend first.

November 23 · Remember those that helped you when you didn't have...

November 22 · I'm just thankful to be here. Not because of who I am or what I do, but celebrating how I was created to serve.

November 21 · I'm just thankful to God for the audacity to believe.

November 11 · I consistently remind myself that it may seem like you are the only one doing what you do and no one notices, but just stick with it. Your gift will make room for you. Even if everything else has to be tried first... who you are and what you do cannot nor will not be denied, especially when you are the one that is uniquely gifted to deliver it.

November 5 · You know I just started thinking about the concept of a "best friend". The interesting thing is that Proverbs talks about a friend loves at all times and if we take that as a basis... we see that when you have a best friend they just simply love you at all times more than others. Not that others don't love you, but a best friend just has a higher impact in commanding the most valuable resource we all have... Time.

October 26 · Character Counts.

October 23 · My cape is a suit.

October 21 · When we finally get really honest with ourselves... We will wake up and realize that some roads we continuously take are in fact dead ends.

October 20 · Too many people deliver on hype while the world is in starvation mode for hope...

October 16 · Everyone wants to learn from and dissect millennials like we are the new science fair project. While this may be true... I would actually turn my attention towards the 'baby boomers' and the little often recognized 'silent generation' because as we all know... 'there is nothing new under the sun, everything did has already been done.' Yes, technology and rapid dissemination of information has ramped us up to unheard of levels of change... But, you still may want to ask someone who's been around the block a time or two...

October 15 · The hustle... It's called The Halo Effect. When you are seen as successful in one area, it's an automatic assumption that the same rules apply in any additional ventures you undertake. It's the power of branding.

October 13 · I believe in the power of Social Media, but at some point your protest must make progress or you will regress from a digress and be in distress.

October 13 · If Playboy ain't getting naked anymore, what do you think this says about society and where we are as a culture?!? *Here's the thing:* When you have access... it's too easy for excess. Once you open so many doors... the funny thing is that the edgy ones are now the ones with standards and restraint.

October 5 · Don't imitate. Innovate! You can't be me better than I can... And I can't be you better than you can.

October 5 · From the prison to the palace... One of my favorite stories in the Bible is that of Joseph. Loved by his father. Sold into slavery by his own brothers. Falsely accused of raping a woman. Thrown into jail. Accurately interpreted the dreams for two of Pharaohs' servants and even after one of them was set free, he was still locked in jail for another two years. After some time, he was called up to interpret the dream for Pharaoh then was made second-in-command of Egypt and saved an entire nation from starvation. I say all of this to say... whether you see this as an improbable tale or even if you see it like one of Aesop's Fables... The story here is very interesting. You got a dude who was a dreamer that was betrayed by his own family, lied on and still maintained character. How many times have we all tried to keep it real when everything went wrong? Get to the point to where you become so good that they can't ignore you and realize that you may go through something, but the key is that you go through... not stop, stay and be stuck.

October 4 · This just hit me like a ton of bricks in the driveway of my house... The reason why things aren't working in any of our lives the way we hope for them to is because we don't believe that the promises that were mentioned are written directly to and for each one of us. When we understand that everything in life is ours for the taking... It begins to strip away the mindset of I'll never have... to a spiritual understanding of I already possess. God is personal. And when we see that it takes the limits off of everything. It's not that we've been restrained by any outside force of God or otherwise, but rather we've been constrained by our own limited thinking of what is truly possible.

September 27 · Until we speak real truth and assassinate the lies... people will forever be lost in their own way of flawed thinking.

September 27 · Don't be so quick to side with just any and every body over any and every thing. Many times when people are being beaten down and attacked, that is the best moment you can take to help them stand up.

September 21 · Every brand is a business, but every business isn't a brand.

September 18 · The setup is to get you to quit. To have you abort every dream inside of you. Here's a message... Don't.

September 17 · When you start to see your problems as an opportunity for growth... You'll begin to see that what was sent to destroy you, truly made you stronger.

September 15 · The streets are always watching. So if you know they're looking... What are you pointing them to?!?

September 13 · One phone call... One email... Can literally change your entire life. Don't feel like you are so stuck in a bad situation that you can't experience breakthrough in one split second. #HopeAgainstHope. #OnlyBelieve

September 11 · My Response is no longer WHY?!? But rather... Thank You. It took me a minute to get here... I just had 50 million questions as to why things were headed the way they were and in many moments felt alone and if I had been abandoned or whatever. I was mad (using G-rated descriptions) and angry, but had a moment this morning where it was all settled with "I Trust You." That everything I've gone through has prepared me for what's next. That I will no longer be anxious for the next thing, but rather enjoy the right now. Yes, this is a growth process but when you get to the point of being able to stand regardless of what is thrown at you, that is the development of character and strength. As any metalworker knows you have to temper materials before you can build with them. Meaning you will be tried by fire, but you will come out without the smell of smoke.

September 10 · I am not moved by my circumstances... I move them! What may seem like an insurmountable task at the time is merely a stepping stone in the right direction.

September 9 · Have people who will see, know and understand all your flaws and regardless of the situation... still believe the best about you.

August 31 · What are you willing to believe?!?

August 31 · Just because you have status, it doesn't mean that you have substance... There is a difference between gold & gold-plated.

August 30 · The thing about friendship is that it is a bond wherein you become willing and vulnerable enough to look out for someone else with nothing more than the intention of protecting their best interest as the center for your actions.

August 28 · When it's the Word vs. the World... Don't take the 'L'.

August 20 · People celebrate the leaves on the tree as they provide shade from the sun, but no one knows what it was like to dig the hole, plant the seed and wait for it to grow.

August 20 · There is a difference between character and convenience.

August 19 · There are no short cuts to winning the race called your life. You have to walk it out... you have to see it through.

August 6 · It just feels good just to come through for people. Regardless of the outcome... Always give it the best that you have.

July 30 · Right now I'm trippin'... 3 years ago when I was working on the JR Crickets project (local Atlanta chicken franchise), I coined the phrase "Flappy Hour" with a launch. Idea was shot down for reasons I won't go into, but yesterday it was a national campaign rollout for Pizza Hut. Not mad... it just validates that the gift inside of you is worth something and you have to protect what is yours. Hold on to those things that you know are true.

July 25 · What I thought was important... Isn't that important anymore.

July 25 · There is something to be said about being tossed into a situation where you think you are unprepared, but in reality you were ready the entire time.

July 9 · The problem with being a "princess" is that many people never pay attention and/or care if and when you ever become a "queen" especially as it relates to the music industry.

July 8 · I can't do anything with a lie.

July 5 · The greater the battle... The greater the victory.

June 22 · You never know the impact that you have on others by simply being your authentic self. Not only is it a representation of character, but it also says, "You can be trusted to do business."

June 15 · What I do is not unique, but how I do it will blow your mind.

June 13 · Your life is what you make of it...

June 4 · I see beyond my circumstances. You get to a point where better is not just "possible" it's exactly how you live and execute your everyday life.

June 2 · Everyone has their own timeline in life. Realize that where you are is just simply where you are. That doesn't mean you won't be at a new destination tomorrow. It's almost like those maps in the mall.... Where you are now is just a locator...

Find your destination and proceed in the direction of that location.

May 23 · Whether you drive a Ferrari California T or a Toyota Camry if you don't put gas in the vehicle you ain't going nowhere... Apply that to your ideas and see your life change.

May 17 · When everyone is trying so hard to push the envelope... You really stand out when you stand up. There is a reason the word stand is the baseline for standard.

May 17 · There is provision for the vision. If the vision doesn't come first, then you are expecting a supply that essentially you have no need for...

May 9 · If I don't do anything else, but build up a fortress of friendships... I can honestly say that I have truly lived.

May 4 · Accountability is everything.

May 4 · You have to know, understand and develop your own unique gifting. We all have them in some way shape or form and many times they show up in multiple areas of our lives. But here's the kicker... Don't get into the trap of comparison because you will begin to obsess over what you don't have rather than cultivate what you do.

April 30 · The days are long, but the years are short...

April 27 · It's not what you say, it's what they hear...

April 27 · People who fail will give you ten reasons why...

April 19 · I think it means something to still go after a dream even after many people have told you no. It must say something when people don't give up. Sometimes it takes a little bit of crazy to live the life that you want.

April 6 · Remember, it's okay to dream... But most people forget to "wake up" and go live the life they saw. That's my Motivation Monday... relentlessly pursue every good thing that has been planned and set aside specifically for you. Don't have a mindset that says you can never do, have or achieve XYZ... Realize a promise has been made and the backer is good for fulfilling everything He said.

April 6 · Happiness is achieved when your dreams become your reality!

April 4 · Every announcement is not grand in nature. Many times my actions say far more than I ever could.

March 30 · "You got yo' hand out for a handout..."

March 30 · Focus on the destination. Forget about the distance.

March 26 · Dream. Then... Do.

March 23 · Give yourself permission to be great.

March 17 · Hey... Don't forget how dope YOU are! Many times we focus on other people and forget we've been blessed and graced with talents of our own.

March 17 · ...He won't let my faith fail.

March 11 · It is not my responsibility to accept the identity of someone else's opinion.

March 11 · We must be willing to win.

February 25 · If you do what you say you do and you are as good as you say are... then the results are inevitable.

February 25 · Sometimes some things just need to be said. Not that anything is expected, but simply that the words must be expressed.

February 19 · What you meant for evil, God meant for my good. I was built for this… I don't quit. I conquer.

February 6 · Before you can do something, you must be something.

February 6 · One idea can make you rich.

February 3 · Amazing conversations happen when you deal with people fueled by passion.

January 20 · People just seem happier to me… I bet it's the gas prices.

January 19 · Before you die… Make sure you really lived.

January 12 · For all of my marketing and branding minded people… You always have to watch for over accessibility… Especially in industries like fashion and luxury… When everyone has it, who really wants it?

January 6 · Today is called 'The Present' because it is 'A Gift'. Enjoy your Life. Love people and don't take anything for granted.

January 4 · Grace is a filter for foolishness… Because after a while you just get tired of all the dumb stuff…

January 3 · Be thorough. We all must do our due diligence in all that we go to do. It always matters.

January 1 · It means something to have a dream… But it means even more to have a plan. Ideas are grand, but execution is everything.

4: TWO THOUSAND FOURTEEN
"The Year of The Renew"

December 29 · I honestly believe 2015 will be filled with unbelievable experiences of greatness, goodness and favor. Not because any of us deserve it, but simply "just because I love you..."

December 20 · Never come to the table empty handed. Always be ready for an exchange. Too many people have a "free-mium" mindset where they offer absolutely nothing and expect everything. It's one thing if someone is led to support you, but don't coerce them with manipulation.
#RulesOfEngagement

December 15 · You can't buy real friends. The price of loyalty costs way too much!

December 11 · Where excellence is not demanded, mediocrity will set in.

December 7 · People ain't perfect. Love them anyway.

November 11 · The most powerful prayer you can pray is 'Thank You'.

October 29 · It is easy to know how many seeds are in an apple. The great mystery is to know how many apples are in a seed.

October 28 · Sometimes it just feels good to kick it with your friends.

October 26 · I will push you, but I will not pull you... It is not my job to get you where you are not really trying to go.

October 25 · Eagles. Soar.

October 23 · People are going to be okay.

October 20 · Time is going to pass whether you take advantage of it or not...

October 8 · Never lose hope.

October 8 · Today, I'm going to be great. I'd like it if you'd join me.

October 8 · Sometimes it is truly hard to face your failures, but once you get past the fear of them...

you become empowered to excel in unimaginable ways.

October 8 · Meek not weak. Humility will raise you. Love will save you. Peace will keep you.

October 5 · I have a Big Dream.

October 1 · The greatest threat to any organization is a lack of leadership. Be a leader. Leadership is lacking in so many places. Business needs it just as much as Family. A leader is not always the loudest, but he/she is the one that people listen to.

September 29 · You can have it all... But don't lose your family in the process.

September 29 · Don't get scared... Many times you're on the right track.

September 29 · My thought process: Many people are trying to buy a house... I'm going after an island. Awaken the visions you let slumber so long ago... They were put in you for a reason.

September 29 · Many times we reflect negative images and mindsets that others have cast upon us. Never get in the position to where you let another person's opinion become your expressed identity.

September 26 · Skills and talent are great, but they are nothing without character and commitment.

September 24 · It is always a pleasure for me to comment on the greatness of other people.

September 24 · That 1 > 10.

September 22 · What does it mean to be free?

September 22 · Thoughts sparked over lunch… this next generation will not be subject to soap operas. I can't even remember how many times we had to be quiet (while playing outside) because of Victor on the Young and the Restless.

September 21 · On days like this… I take drives with the windows down singing Prince songs at the top of my lungs hitting every single high note… #EnjoyYourLife

September 21 · At some point… You just believe it.

September 18 · Sometimes you just see things before other people…

September 17 · Purpose is a catalytic word.

September 17 · I think people have always had a sense of rebellion. The question is what do you do when you can no longer act out because that is the norm? Watch what's next.

September 16 · A ninja never carries a business card. If you really do what you say you do... We'll know...

September 13 · When people tell you, "Wow! You've lost some weight..." what they're really saying is... "You're not as fat as you used to be." Presentation is everything. It's all in how you say it.

September 11 · The world has changed a lot the past 13 years. In what was a catastrophic tragedy in the lives that were lost, I give thanks for the bonds that were forged amongst all people in spite of. It is truly Amazing Grace that what would most see as our weakest point as a country, only resolved us to remember that we truly are: One Nation. Under God. Indivisible. With Liberty and Justice for All...

September 7 · Your mindset is your mind set.

September 7 · It means something to have a standard.

August 19 · An American beheading across the world and uproar across the street. This doesn't require political, racial or religious debates to see that there are indeed problems. 2 American deaths played out on the world's stage are only the most recent in a line of senseless actions and at some point we have to say no more. It doesn't take a rallying cry of a mass multitude of people, but rather each one of us making a personal commitment to live a life of love. Division is a tactic (Divide & Conquer), but love is a choice (Unbreakable Bond).

August 18 · A trend will bend, but a brand will stand.

August 18 · Saddest thing about creativity is that there is such a lack of it people will mimic instead of invent.

August 18 · Have you ever been kicked in the teeth chasing after your dreams? Good. Next time recover faster...

August 18 · I dreamed a dream, but then I made it my reality.

August 16 · People before Product will yield Profit on your Projects.

August 16 · What you don't know about me is my love for fighting games. Especially Marvel vs. Capcom 2. I can't count the quarters spent at Tilt or the overnights at Funsville for this game. Kids don't know what it's like to claim next with a quarter or token...

August 14 · You will forever be frustrated trying to fit in when you are destined to stand out.

August 13 · You have to realize... in certain situations the best response is: "No comment."

August 7 · Thank you to all the people that allow me to dream. It means more than you know.

August 6 · When you know who are, you'll better realize what you will and won't tolerate...

August 1 · Learn the landscape.

July 28 · Create your own reality.

July 27 · We were all put on this planet to make a difference in the lives of others. Love is by far one of the coolest things to ever experience.

July 26 · Be salt. Not salty.

July 22 · When you understand that you don't have to become what you already are, you shift from negative mindset into an established authority.

July 19 · Sometimes the best thing you can do is listen.

July 18 · To a famished man, anything bitter is sweet.

July 17 · I'm unwilling to compromise. And for some reason, I just think that means something.

July 17 · Believe to be better.

July 15 · Faith fixes anything.

July 9 · Be Free.

July 6 · The Word of God is a love letter to us on how to be successful in life.

July 2 · Whatever it takes to figure it out and move forward... That is my resolve.

July 2 · A logo is not a brand.

July 2 · Leadership is Life.

July 1 · Know your worth. True quality never goes on sale.

July 1 · The mind is like an ocean. The deepest thoughts may appear to be shallow.

June 29 · Keep people in your life who care enough to point out your greatness even when you are stuck on your flaws.

June 27 · It amazes me at how many people don't realize that they can live the life of their dreams. As a heads up it is a step-by-step process, but can be strategically planned and executed. To say it's not hard would be a boldface lie, but it is possible and is worth it.

June 27 · You can't evolve into what you won't explore.

June 23 · I have dined at some of the best restaurants in the country, but ain't nothin' like a Chick-fil-a cookies n' creme milkshake.

June 21 · Learn your lane and master it.

June 21 · The vision is the blueprint given to experience the life of your dreams.

June 16 · "Yesterday you said tomorrow." – Nike Ad

June 14 · Entrepreneurship- French word meaning, 'one who creates something new.'

June 14 · 'Tell me and I'll forget. Show me and I'll remember. Involve me and I'll understand.' - Chinese Proverb

June 14 · Just something I'd thought I'd share with you all... a cup of coffee typically costs about $0.07.

Think about that the next time you go to Starbucks. The power of a branded experience… Fraps on deck.

June 13 · You can't change people. Either accept them for who they are or keep it moving. When they are ready to change, they will. And the best thing you can do is encourage them all along the way.

June 11 · In the midst of a storm… be a palm tree. Bend, but don't break.

June 10 · It took a minute, but I had to get back to me. It's amazing at how we can custom create self-inflicted detours…

June 10 · At one point… I remember love being considered weak, but the truth is, now I realize it's the strongest thing that has ever existed.

June 7 · I fully believe that you have to do what you have to do and in all truth… I've done a lot. But a sign holder/waver in the Georgia heat…

June 5 · I wonder if "Back That Thing Up" will ever be played on the true oldies station… It is a classic.

May 29 · I'm just built differently than most. I refuse to settle and I'm okay with that.

May 24 · If you don't like it, change it or your perception of it.

May 22 · This literally just came to me: "I can't PURGE my PURPOSE because it fuels my PASSION that creates my POSITION for my PLACE of PROMOTION."

May 22 · If you dream big enough, people gonna think you're crazy... Well call me a lunatic. If you believe hard enough, people gonna think you're stupid... Well consider me dumb. And if you stay with it long enough, you'll come out with everything that you were promised. Then people will ask how did you do it... 1 word: Grace.

May 15 · So I was recently challenged with the question: "What would happen if you gave something everything that you had?" And so I made a commitment to commit and literally my life changed overnight. If you've never been asked that question I dare you to answer it right now.

May 13 · You keep praying to God for trees, but refuse to plant the acorns you already have.

May 12 · Commit to Commitment.

May 12 · Talent without commitment is nothing more than an empty vapor of semi-permanent entertainment.

May 11 · You can physically take everything I have. But you cannot take my mind.

May 10 · Do exactly what you were called to do. No one can take that from you.

May 10 · Step Back to Step Up. Sometimes it's necessary.

May 10 · Don't lose hope.

May 10 · You will always go where you are thinking.

May 10 · Hardest thing to change is your mind, but once you do the previous limitations are removed.

May 8 · Excellence is an art. It is the consistent dedication to execution at the highest level of one's greatest abilities.

May 5 · Action without direction is motion with no movement.

May 5 · One of the greatest detriments to a company's success is a lack of leadership.

May 5 · Your mind is a thermostat. Stop using it as a thermometer. It is not your job to check the temperature. Your job is to set it.

May 3 · I can create faster than you can copy.

May 3 · When I think about it... Branding and I have been friends for a very long time.

April 28 · If the dream isn't big enough... Make it bigger.

April 27 · We are what we decide to be...

April 27 · Take action. Feel the fear and do it anyway.

April 24 · That's right, "these girls ain't loyal." But let's be honest for a moment... was she even a woman of substance and of high quality character in the first place? I'd venture to say that, "those particular girls are loyal." So before we further deteriorate the already strained male/female relationships, let's give a fair assessment and fully evaluate the prospects in the selection beforehand.

April 20 · When it's custom, it counts.

April 20 · Too many people have motion with no movement.

April 20 · My mom just used "or nah" in an Easter Sunday text message. #done

April 8 · It's kinda cool experiencing this thing call life. I've watched as my friends have turned into fathers and with that, their level of commitment to other people has increased. Growing up is cool. Getting "old" is not. Always stay fresh, playa.

April 8 · Toms are nothing more than some burlap bedroom shoes, but they are comfortable...

April 5 · There are many things that can be substituted in branding, but cereal is one of those things where you have to get the real deal.

March 30 · Business plans can be copied, but a brand is unique and original. I like to call it being #RAWthentic.

March 25 · Just saw a dude face plant at the gas station. Only thing I could think of was "Walk it off, playa. Just walk it off..."

March 25 · Interesting dynamic when we finally realize that we are the ones that need to recognize the true strength we've already been given...

March 24 · The world is mine.

March 22 · When you are ready to change... you will.

March 21 · Use resources. Not people.

March 18 · Learning how to be nice... My grandmother is so wise.

March 16 · Looking for Love? It's much easier to find someone after you've found yourself.

March 15 · It is not my job to make my name great.

March 13 · Depression is nothing more than anger turned inward... You are feeling this way simply because you have bought the lie of being stuck and frustrated, but the reality is that you are free as you believe.

March 5 · I'm tired of amateurs claiming to be experts.

March 3 · Time to switch it up on 'em once again...

February 28 · If you build your own system, you'll never be dependent on theirs...

February 26 · Cheap people...

February 22 · I think country musicians are some of the best storytellers in the music industry. There is an interesting parallel between them and lyrical hip-hop artists.

February 22 · Learning how, but never doing is a complete waste of time.

February 22 · Do what is necessary to succeed.

February 21 · It is as easy to be great as to be small.

February 20 · Conquer the Mind. Conquer the World.

February 15 · You have to be and stay around people that are going places and have been somewhere. When you are exposed to new things it takes you to a next-level playing field and I'll tell you firsthand, once you go up... there is no reason to come back down.

February 15 · No one can TAKE what you freely GIVE... I used to be so concerned with people taking advantage of me and my creative abilities that I would isolate myself. In truth that was an act of fear because I was afraid I would run out. But when I realized that I wasn't the source it opened my entire world. Now I'm not saying be stupid and give everything you have away, but in Business, Life and Love, you should always GIVE the other person or party the advantage.

February 11 · You forget Whitney Houston is gone, but you never will forget her Voice.

February 9 · My gift is not for me.

February 8 · Get back up again.

February 8 · Money Buys You Time.

February 4 · Free Your Time.

January 31 · Go Forward.

January 31 · The ballad of the secret Christian... maleness vs. manhood.

January 31 · Stay Focused.

January 31 · More money = More options. Like Willie Hutch... I Choose You.

January 29 · Displaced Desire Declares Disaster.

January 17 · Have you ever just been happy? Not because of anyone else, but just because you are in control of your own life?!? That's real peace.

January 17 · Success is planned and time is short. Make moves that make sense. Or be the victim of your own laziness...

January 17 · I am Tony Rouse. So many people have no idea of who they are. They live life as other people, but haven't taken the time to learn themselves. A major point of freedom is knowing that God loves you, but an even bigger step forward is knowing that He actually likes you. It'll also greatly help if you begin to think about yourself in the same way.

January 16 · Make a promise to yourself. Others will let you down, but hold yourself up. That's real love.

January 7 · Successful people "grow" to the next level...

5: TWO THOUSAND THIRTEEN
"The Year of The Reset"

December 29 · Love your neighbor as thyself… You can't love someone more than you love yourself. You also can't give what you do not have. Charity starts at home.

December 28 · Raise Your Standards. What you accept is what you allow…

December 22 · For those that don't know the rules… Christmas Card = Inner Circle. You don't just hand-write an address when a text message will do.

December 15 · Are you a pigeon or an eagle? The difference is walking around picking through trash vs. Soaring to new heights.

December 13 · I'm not comfortable being comfortable.

December 9 · Don't ever tell me something is impossible when I've seen someone else do it... and if I haven't seen anyone else do it, it's probably meant for me to make it a reality for others.

December 5 · Are You a Winner or a Whiner?

December 5 · A title doesn't make you a leader... It merely affords you the opportunity to become one. Many people have no clue what it means to lead. They get into a position and flop. You can lead right from where you are now.

December 1 · One of the most important things to me is having people around that I can't do anything for... These are the people that see and know the real you. They have been granted access simply because they accept you for who you are and their perception is based on the person, not the performance.

November 14 · I'd rather spend an extra $5 today on healthier food options than spend $50K on surgeries 20 years down the road...

November 12 · What are the 3 things you want in life? This is an example of one of the questions you should ask yourself as you are preparing for greatness.

November 12 · Be mindful of who you share your dreams with! Everyone will not be excited as you are. Ask Joseph...

November 11 · Clothes don't make the man... but they DO introduce him!

November 11 · Many people suffer from a lack of leadership...

November 4 · I've had some of the best spiritual encounters with those people who would seem to be the most secular. Don't be so deep that you can't be reached...

October 31 · All of my closest friends had some of the most major changes in their life this year... and we ain't done yet...

October 31 · WTF (Where's the Faith)?!? If you don't believe it... you'll never receive it, see it or be it!

October 29 · A message for businesses across America... Doing something unimportant well does not make it more important. (You're just efficient at things that don't really matter...)

October 28 · Rich people yell. Wealthy people whisper. Be mindful of individuals making random noise...

October 28 · When people ask what is it that I do... To put it simply: I solve problems.

October 27 · There is no such thing as thinking too big! The problem is that you are around too many people that think too small... Don't ever let other people's failure become your reality.

October 27 · Regardless of what it looks like... You can't shake me. I've been through too much to fall apart now...

October 19 · No Trespassing: Everyone should not have access to you. Filter your friends...

October 19 · If your current circle of friends isn't pushing you for growth, reassess your association...

October 19 · Your dreams are possible. They are very tangible. Don't ever believe the lie that your life has no purpose and that you don't matter. You do and it does... Dare to Dream. Success is Real. Pursue Your Passion. I lost everything and gained all I ever needed at the same time. It ain't easy, but I'm so much better because of it.

October 18 · I thrive... Not just survive.

October 13 · Open your "eyes"... see by faith and not by natural sight.

October 13 · Revelation brings Revolution.

October 11 · It is important for me to be successful, but I am also glad that I have friends of whose successes I can be a part of. Success has many forms… whether it's being a parent, getting married, owning a home or even showcasing your art, I'm happy to be able to be a part of each of your lives. You all push me to be better… Thank You. The Littlest things oftentimes make the biggest impact…

October 10 · It's not so much that I'm cut from a different cloth, but rather I think on a much higher plane…

October 7 · Don't let good enough be good enough. This is how you have to see your life. There is vast difference between good and great!

October 7 · You have enough people against you… Don't be against yourself…

October 4 · Examine your circle… My destiny is too important to be connected to people who aren't going anywhere.

September 29 · Planning for today is too late! Everything is not an emergency.

August 31 · Free branding advice: Jacksonville needs to get Tim Tebow. I'm speaking from the perspective of an owner. Ticket sales would increase and that creates a budget to upgrade players. It just makes sense...

August 29 · There is no Plan B. Success is the only option. Live your wildest dreams. Follow through. Execute in Business, Money, Love, Life and Relationships. Be happy every day. Adventure awaits. Love God. Love People.

August 27 · Beware of the Dreamkillers. Everyone can't handle your vision. Learn this quickly... Any relationship that doesn't support your calling should be cut off.

August 21 · A Mufasa Moment: The time in a man's life when he stops singing 'Hakuna Matata' and takes his rightful place as king.

August 21 · Be a River. Not a Reservoir.

August 19 · Many people have suggestions... Very few have answers.

August 17 · The best thing you can do to impact other people's lives... is to Love them. Life Lessons on Living. This is Honest Truth. Love is the strongest force on this planet. Only when you submit to it, will you experience its True Power.

August 14 · People with large amounts of disposable income often have low amounts of disposable time. Makes you think about those people that swear they are stacking chips, but are never busy...

August 13 · I can't speak for Drake, but when I went to new levels... all of my 'Old Friends' didn't make it...

August 13 · Stop putting a Band-Aid on something that requires surgery.

August 7 · Too many people are comfortable being extra-average when you were called to be extraordinary!!!

August 7 · At some point you have to look in the mirror and say... "You are the problem."

August 7 · I don't know what I don't know... but I'm willing to learn.

August 6 · When you are quiet... You begin to make the most noise.

August 6 · My thoughts... Say It 'til You See It.

August 5 · Believe.

August 5 · Dominate.

August 3 · Who you are is far more important than what you can do...

August 2 · Anyone can change when they finally decide to...

July 31 · Many struggle to achieve external power, but the truth is... when you understand your internal power, the struggle ceases to exist.

July 29 · God, Dam It. (Isaiah 59:9 - The Original Text: When the enemy comes in like a flood, God will lift up a standard.) I personally think we easily get too stuck and stiff. Life is meant to be lived and we have to trust God that when we get hit from all sides he'll block every attack and keep us safe.

July 29 · Poverty was meant to destroy you.

July 27 · Don't base your success off of the failure of others. Just because they didn't make it... it doesn't mean that you can't.

July 26 · Life will gladly kick your butt as long as you will let it.

July 23 · How easily are you distracted? Why?

July 22 · What do you really want? Why do you want it? Who do you want it for?

July 22 · In the process of feeding other people... you sometimes forget that you need to eat.

July 18 · In life... Play Chess. Pawns move before The King and Queen.

July 16 · People are doing too much in social media. These unfriend/unfollow threats are excessive. The reality: people have different backgrounds, beliefs and understanding. If the channel for dialogue isn't available how will you ever grow? I'm definitely not saying tolerate stupidity and unfiltered ignorance, but many times people will listen to what you have to say when you speak with them and not at them.

July 15 · Upgrade Yourself.

July 13 · You swear you're a Boss... but in reality... you're a customer at best. The next step is employee... Know that everyone is somewhere and can move up, but be honest with where you are now and then go from there. We'll know by your moves not your announcements.

July 13 · When your target market is everyone you will fail.

July 13 · I had a conversation with a deaf gentleman today. He said no words, but his actions spoke to my heart. So often we mistake molehills for mountains. It's not your problems... It's how you view them.

July 7 · People say what they won't do, but in most cases when the price is right... They will still buy.

July 6 · Lose Your Religion. Build a Relationship.

July 5 · Confidence will get you everything.

July 3 · You don't know what it took to get me here. Everyone has a story.

July 2 · Finishing is better than Starting. It's easy to start... the question is will you finish???

July 1 · I won't settle for 2nd place.

July 1 · When I changed for other people... It never worked out.

June 30 · People want the picture of success, but refuse to go through the process.

June 29 · A friend will accept you as you are... A true friend will push you to be better.

June 27 · Communication is key... Women need Love. Men need Respect.

June 26 · Don't ruin your future marriage by playing hurtful games.

June 23 · Just because something is widely accepted... it doesn't mean it's true.

June 23 · God Loves You... I spent my entire weekend outside, sleeping on the ground and loved every minute of it.

June 13 · There is no substitute for Bacon.

June 11 · I lift up my hands. I didn't learn success until I understood surrender.

June 11 · Look Up...

June 6 · Check the resume... I'm not new to this, I'm true to this.

June 6 · When 411 don't know and 911 can't help... 'Call Jesus'... He is on the Mainline.

June 6 · Theory is for the Weary. If it works so well, then why are you not doing it?!? Give me somebody who has been somewhere.

June 5 · Love is a verb.

June 5 · Light shines brightest in the deepest darkness.

June 5 · Go for the deeper, not the cheaper. True quality never goes on sale.

June 5 · Math 101: Seed + Time = Harvest

June 5 · The greatest thing you will ever make in life is a decision.

June 4 · When I stopped lying to myself, I stopped lying to other people.

June 4 · Branding is my muse. Creation my addiction. Do not be confused, Marketing's my mission.

June 4 · You cannot fight what you will not face.

April 23 · SOAR. So much meaning behind that one word... It's a rallying cry for all Eagles, but most importantly it is a commandment.

April 23 · God has blessed my life with some amazing people. I oftentimes forget how many of you have supported me throughout the years. From the times when I recruited you guys to paint Electric Blue Signs for E-Squad, paid you in Pizza or even had you up hanging sheet signs... I am truly thankful for your time, support and energy.

April 18 · Today's branding lesson: People buy you before they buy your product...

March 25 · Think Big. Aim High. Trust God.

March 25 · Stay Humble. Stay Patient. Stay Focused.

March 22 · When it comes to style, it's always all about the details.

March 22 · Never settle.

March 21 · Money talks... And cash still has the biggest mouthpiece.

March 19 · I don't compete. I dominate.

March 14 · I am awake.

March 13 · Stay 30 steps ahead...

March 7 · You never realize how truly unhappy you were until you get happy.

February 26 · Design.

February 26 · "Time is the most valuable thing one can spend." -Theophrastus

February 24 · You want to miss God's purpose for your life? Live in Envy of other people. Live to please other people. Envy- I must be like you to be happy. People Pleasing- I must be liked by you to be happy.

February 24 · If you live by the approval of others, you will die by their rejection.

February 23 · The hardest thing you will ever make in life is a decision. The rest of it is simple follow through.

February 18 · It makes no sense to do what rich people do when you haven't completed the process of what made them rich. Go back and acknowledge the path that helped them get there. Had to learn this one myself...

February 18 · The key to success? START with a plan.

February 18 · I work VERY well with people who know their role and stay in their lane.

February 18 · I am the CEO of my life.

February 17 · Let your yes be yes and your no be no. #PowerfulStatement

February 16 · When you know that you own something... You never have to chase it.

February 16 · I never realized how much I've been inspired and influenced by The Cosby Show.

February 14 · My mind will forever stay free.

February 13 · It has been said that people don't change. That is a lie. The complete truth is that people don't change themselves.

January 30 · Just because I don't, doesn't mean I can't because when I do you'll wish I didn't.

January 28 · Don't be a victim of manufactured intimacy. Get a relationship so you can experience the real thing.

January 28 · There is no one that can stop Tony Rouse, but Tony Rouse.

January 27 · Something so profound just hit me... You can't see in the dark! That phrase right there will create a mind shift if you think about it.

January 27 · Love is not what I have... It's who I am.

January 27 · Tony's Top 5 Animated Movies: 1.) Happy Feet 2.) The Incredibles 3.) Aladdin 4.) The Lion King 5.) Beauty & the Beast

January 25 · The worst thing you can be in life is CHEAP!

January 14 · This Justin Timberlake #Suit&Tie is sounding like a dope soundtrack for the fellas for 2013. Marketing has shifted to cater more to men and it's time that Guys are guys again. Just watch...

6: TWO THOUSAND TWELVE
"The Year of The Revive"

December 15 · I love my people! We are at this gala and tickets are $500+ a piece... And we are tearing this floor up with the electric slide in tuxedos and furs...

November 26 · Life is an open book test, but don't forget that you have already been given the answer key. #ReadYourBible

November 20 · The most powerful thing you can ever make is a decision.

November 20 · You may be a male, but only maturity can make you a man.

November 19 · There was a point in my life when I desired external gratification. Now my focus is to simply live as a man of character, integrity and love.

November 18 · I will take quality over quantity any day of the week.

November 16 · Everybody WANTS something. I'm determined to BE something.

November 16 · When you have the mindset of a winner, there is nothing that can shake you. Even when the outlook seems to be grim, that champion focused mindset will bring you to, bring you through and set you up for the next success.

November 16 · You've already been promised victory... Act like it.

November 14 · Stevie Wonder = Real Musician

November 13 · New Years is almost here. Make a resolution to change now (if you need to) so that when the clock strikes... its already a habit.

November 13 · "Do not think that what is hard for you to master is humanly impossible; and if it is humanly possible, consider it to be within your reach." — Marcus Aurelius

November 11 · I'm even more inspired to be successful. Not simply in the traditional sense, but in the way God has called me to be. I've never been average (best of the worst, worst of the best) and I'm thankful for my brothers like Will Fogleman and Zion Birdsong for keeping me sharp. #ironmen

November 11 · Growth is necessary.

November 8 · People always ask me: "So what do you do?!?" My response always seemed to vary. I finally found a title and an occupation. My role you ask... Creative Consultant.

November 7 · Nothing just happens. In life you have two options... Be effective or affected.

November 6 · Dear Jesus... I know where I've been. Thank God you didn't let me stay there.

November 5 · God is for me.

October 19 · It is the simple things we must remember and commit to understanding. You will never get to 50 Million without securing 50 Thousand.

October 16 · "You can't love an insecure person out of their insecurities. They... THEY NEED to do some work on themselves." I've been on both sides of this coin. Change doesn't happen until you do.

October 16 · When I realized God wasn't in a hurry to fix my problems, I stopped creating them.

October 16 · Character is the foundation for greatness.

October 15 · You want a successful life? Start here: 1.) Make a promise and keep it. 2.) Set a goal and work to achieve it.

October 15 · I can't change you, but I can change me and what I'm willing to tolerate.

October 15 · When your feelings control your actions, it is because you have given up control.

October 15 · Love is a verb.

October 15 · Who you are shouts so loudly in my ears I cannot hear what you say.

October 15 · If there is little or no trust, there is no foundation for permanent success.

October 15 · Money can't buy loyalty. That's a character trait.

October 15 · Your power lies in your ability to say no.

October 15 · What you say and do is reflection of who you are.

October 14 · The worst thing to ever be told is that you have potential. It means that you have more that you're capable of, but in some way unwilling to demonstrate it.

October 10 · Purpose is not found within the creation, but with the Creator.

October 9 · It all begins with an idea...

October 8 · EVERYTHING is based on SEED, TIME and HARVEST. You are where you are as a result of the previous decisions you have made. Good news is you can change your course and get different results. How? Look at what you are planting...

September 17 · Better is always possible. Set a new goal and dream a new dream. Don't just imagine the possibilities... Plan them.

September 17 · Attack. Sometimes the boldest of offenses come from the most reserved demeanor. Always watch out for the quiet ones...

September 15 · Kids are funny. Spent the day with my 13 yr. old mentee and learned a great deal about life from the mind of an eighth grader. I almost had to ask who's training who... Best dude in the world.

September 15 · I love how people move to tell me that they are the best, but I reserve my thoughts to think that if you were... the proper exchange would be me telling you.

September 13 · Only believe.

September 12 · Know WHO you ARE.

September 12 · Sometimes it's just not worth it...

September 12 · One word of encouragement can drastically change your outlook on life.

September 10 · Submitted and committed.

September 8 · You know there really are some lost people in this world who just need help. If you are a person who believes in, knows and just simply trusts God, then get on your job... If you just live your life to help people as opposed to pointing fingers at them, you'll find that it's much more rewarding. #SaturdaySoapbox

September 3 · Development sucks, but is necessary. You must enjoy the journey as you embark upon your destination. I'll tell you, I've never been so strong and so weak at the same time. Weak in my own strength, but strong in the love of God. Took a while to even understand this, but I know the results will be nothing short of worth it. Pressing on...

September 1 · Thank God for football.

August 28 · Don't energize your enemies.

August 26 · It is impossible to turn a negative thought into a positive action.

August 25 · Love is our greatest need. Rejection is our greatest fear.

August 24 · Just be happy.

August 24 · When you have vision... You have victory. #lifelonglove

August 24 · You don't want friends that will make you feel comfortable; you want friends who will challenge you to a good life. #lifelonglove

August 24 · Play another slow jam, this time make it sweet.

August 23 · Sitting on my patio listening to the rain. Peace is one of those things that money can't buy, but you'd pay whatever the cost to have it.

August 23 · In your life, have and maintain a set standard. It's worth it to your future.

August 23 · The power of silence.

August 20 · Tough times don't last... Tough people do.

August 14 · "I will never give you a 2nd place prize when you put me 1st." – God

August 13 · "An intelligent man will open your mind. A handsome man will open your eyes. A gentleman will open your heart." -Dr. Farrah Gray

August 13 · The song "His Eye is on The Sparrow". The meaning and reference comes from Matthew 10:29. *Meaning:* If a monetarily invaluable bird is important to God, then how much more are you important to him?!? I got up this morning and observed some birds. They literally have no cares. They are free to do whatever they want and keep it moving. That's a powerful representation of our capabilities that we have in this life.

August 13 · It seems as if I've had to press the reset button...

August 13 · No is not never. Delay is not denial.

August 13 · The most beautiful thing about life is... living.

August 12 · That moment when you have, understand and move into your purpose...

August 11 · 4 years ago, I was learning how to walk again from having both of my legs broken. This morning I ran sprints. Replay your victories.

June 18 · Stop focusing on what you are not. Start focusing on who you are.

June 13 · You have the ability to make a lasting impact on people whether you realize it or not.

May 29 · Stay bitter or get better.

May 23 · I am finally beginning to understand the necessity of a simple life. Life itself is not complex, but rather we make it so as we place a weighted importance upon unimportant things.

May 18 · Be mindful of what goes in your eyes and ears. At some point, it will come out of your mouth.

May 7 · Indescribable, uncontainable, you placed the stars in the sky and you know them by name...

May 7 · Choose your friends very carefully. You are the average of the 5 people you associate with the most.

May 4 · It's amazing how you can meet someone that'll point out your faults, but support you in the ability to correct them.

May 4 · I refuse to give up, cave in or quit.

May 3 · I think, therefore I am.

May 2 · An interesting take on life: You want to stay relevant? Always be able to answer the questions, "What's New?" "What's Now?" "What's Next?"

May 2 · If you only are concerned with success defined by other people... be prepared to wear yourself out.

April 15 · There used to be a saying that said, "if you want to hide something from someone, put it in a book." But now with the presence of the internet... We all have no excuse. Decide today to accomplish those dreams that you planned 2, 5, 10 years ago. It's never too late to become who you already are.

April 5 · Every shut eye ain't sleep, every goodbye ain't gone...

7: TWO THOUSAND ELEVEN
"The Year of The Refresh"

December 6 · I think I had the biggest revelation in my life over Thanksgiving. My grandmother simply said, "Be Nice."

November 18 · The weekend started on Thursday. #thingsilearnedincollege

November 17 · A Mogul Move in Atlanta is owning a parking lot. I watched 15 cars park for Soul Train Awards at $20 each. Glad I have VIP parking near the Fox.

November 17 · I used to think I wanted to expand my circle of friends... As I have grown, I understand the goal is to expand my influence.

November 13 · Just saw it go down in Wells Fargo parking lot. Her: "Gimme my hair." Him: "Go get it." (Throws it down.) She picks it up and dusts it off.

November 12 · Can we get to Thanksgiving before you guys roll out with the Christmas Lights?

November 10 · Today I'm converting foresight into insight to avoid hindsight.

November 9 · Success excites me. My mind is filled w/ ideas & dreams I believe are possible. I perfect what others call impossible.

November 8 · Define the important. At the end of the day Nothing Else Matters. So often we give unnecessary attention to things that don't deserve it.

November 5 · You don't have to be overly exposed to be relevant. Look at the success Michael Buble' has experienced & many don't have a clue to who he is.

November 3 · As a kid my favorite holiday was Christmas, but as an adult its Thanksgiving hands down. No shopping, just food, family and fun. #LetsEat

November 2 · Talent and energies shared amongst unappreciative individuals is a waste of time for all.

November 1 · You are the governor of your own limitations. Don't just have a view of limitless possibilities. Make them a reality through action.

October 31 · The key to life: 1.) Love God 2.) Love People. When you strip all the foolishness away, the simple things are all you need.

October 27 · Knowledge is power, but it's also profit.

October 20 · Average simply defined is being the Best of the Worst and the Worst of the Best. The question is how long do you want to dwell in the land of average? We were created to win and win consistently. Is it easy? Actually yes, but not initially. That is why people quit. We are all a part of the microwave generation and expect things at the push of a button. Look at Twitter... its instant information, but when you're plotting out success you have to plan for tomorrow while correcting course today. A simple reality courtesy of Pastor Reginald Ezell: "You can't change your present situation. Your present situation is based on your past choices. You can however change your future outcome by adjusting your present choices." So do yourself a favor... plan for tomorrow, but begin fixing the issue today. Always better to be known as the Best of the Best as opposed to the Best of the Worst.

October 15 · The Reality: A Ninja does not carry business cards. You know his occupation AFTER you've been chopped in back of the throat.

October 15 · Amazing Saturday. Be sure that it's not said that you "SAT-around-all-day"...

October 15 · The reality: Everyone in your life is NOT your friend, BUT when you find those that are... Hang on to them. People without an agenda are rare, but do exist.

September 23 · If you never leave the basics, you never have to go back to them.

September 23 · Stick to the plan. The fundamentals should never change. When they do, change them back.

September 19 · This is the day that the Lord has made and he is concerned about me, and you too...

September 17 · It's possible.

September 13 · A lesson learned... You're not respected until you say "No."

September 11 · It is kinda surreal that you can remember exactly what you were doing 10 years ago when you heard about the World Trade Center.

September 8 · Today, exercise your ability to succeed in everything that you go to do. #GoWithGod

August 28 · Random thoughts in life... Who took the time to create the rhyme, U-G-L-Y you ain't got no alibi, you ugly? Alibi is a big word. I doubt the original creator was 12.

August 27 · Confession: I don't check voicemail. If you know me... text me.

August 26 · I'm in a mindset of expectation. Something good is going to happen to you today. It is so easy to think negatively, but what if the off chance you said the opposite to those negative thoughts and words. Change the way you think; you'll change the way you talk. Change the way you talk; you WILL change your life.

August 19 · I'd rather be a producer than consumer.

August 15 · The more I think I have it all figured out, the further realization I get about having no clue. Life: 4 letter word that is a synonym for roller coaster.

July 26 · When was the last time you gave your time away? Not wasting it, but actually taking a moment to check in with people. I did it over the weekend and realized we all too often get wrapped up in our own world and sometimes it's just a good thing to say "Hey, What Up?" You'll be amazed at how far that little bit of concern will take you.

July 24 · 4 am and what am I doing??? Watching American Gangster. Many lessons learned in this well-written story. Blue Magic.

July 15 · In relationships... it's not the impression (physical), but the impression (spiritual)...

July 15 · I hate when people under-deliver.

July 15 · Had a thought today. My personality and/or character traits have been described in many ways, but I want to develop fearlessness. Not living life with reckless abandonment, but accepting the challenge and succeeding on every level. Think about it. What have we all not accomplished/done because of fear?

July 13 · Make a decision to be great and constantly better your absolute best.

July 8 · Beloved I wish above ALL things that thou mayest prosper and be in health, even as thy soul prosper. *Translation:* Get on Top. Stay on Top. Don't Stop.

July 6 · Growth and Development is crucial to your ultimate success in life.

June 26 · Powerful statements in black history: "You got the juice now."

June 26 · I must accept responsibility and know that even though I put a first AND last name in my phone, I must add descriptions. #WhoAreYou

June 26 · For some reason I was under the impression that becoming an overnight success didn't take over 10 years. #LearnedQuick

June 24 · "Follow me on twitter. Follow me on twitter." My thoughts: you don't lead in real life...

June 24 · Success is 4 things: 1.) Good friends. 2.) Good reputation. 3.) Liking what you do. 4.) Giving back... You are successful.

June 24 · You have to have people skills.

June 24 · "You want to be successful, start pursuing your far-fetched dreams, every day."

June 24 · Dreams are a big deal.

June 24 · Where you start the journey has nothing to do with where you finish. When you start is the most important.

June 19 · Phone call this morning for advice. I don't mind... only providing info from the past things God helped me with. I spit that WORD. #ask

June 14 · Be mindful of the celebration of others' misfortune. You will reap what you sow.

June 14 · Are you excited today? I mean excited so much that you can do nothing but celebrate joy. Smile. It looks good on you.

June 13 · You can always correct course and accomplish great things if you focus on that which is most important.

June 13 · It's an amazing time to be alive. Celebrate the attitude of thankfulness.

June 5 · Be mindful of the company you keep. Sometimes they'll keep you from getting to where you are meant to be.

June 4 · Sometimes you have to leave and figure some things out for a while, but never abandon your dreams.

May 30 · It's amazing what happens when you live life authentically. You realize you make mistakes and learn to correct course. Only thing to do is keep it moving.

May 28 · My ideal life is a combination of American Gangster, Hitch, Passion of the Christ and

Entourage. I want to be wealthy, smart, love God and enjoy life with my friends.

May 27 · Why do we keep piping hot foods in our mouths while they are burning our tongue and cheeks? And try to let extra air in with no avail?

May 18 · There is nothing like being humbled. The process SUCKS going through it, but afterwards you thank God you did.

May 12 · Ever get the feeling that there are way too many distractions?

May 12 · I remember when we thought AOL instant messenger was the coolest thing ever.

May 12 · You want to stay successful?!? Wake up the first time.

May 11 · "Nobody knows the trouble I've seen. Nobody knows my song." It's amazing how stuck in this mentality we become. EVERYONE has a song. Your resolution is to choose a different tune.

May 10 · "Success is perfected preparation."

April 29 · You have to see it, before you see it, or you're never gonna see it! Yeah it's great that we won Best Social Event, but if you come into my office you'll see my vision board with a picture of an award and the tagline achievement that was up way before the night of the ceremony. Everything that happens in life is a direct result of your thoughts and your words. Put yourself in success' pathway. Make it happen.

April 29 · Seed. Time. Harvest. Same process for everything in life.

April 27 · Looking for something else to conquer... I'm thinking the next may be my own discipline. It's weird how when I go after something I get it, but if you can't control self, what is the point.

April 17 · If you have the opportunity to interact with older generations, don't be so quick to cast them off as not being relevant to today's time. Insight I learned firsthand: You need their wisdom; They need your strength.

March 30 · So many people want to be #1 and that's great, but your attitude to get there is all wrong. People on top serve others. Think about it...

March 28 · It amazing what happens when someone tells you thank you with sincerity. Not that I had to hear it, but because they said it and meant it. Something about someone being grateful. Makes you wanna help over and over again.

March 23 · I created this cycle for my corporate clients that I'll share with you:

Refresh - New Day. New Dreams to accomplish.
Recover - Keep Going. If you slip, gain ground.
Renew - Energize yourself...
Reward - Celebrate the success.
Rewind - Study the correct moves & fine tune errors.
Repeat - Success breeds success.

Make the day great.

March 23 · I believe in excellence. We have accepted mediocrity in almost every area of our lives. When are we going to demand more, not just from others, but most importantly from ourselves? I saw a global ranking this morning that has the U.S. listed as 23rd in Science and 31st in Math and we used to be Top 3! I've made a commitment to be the best in everything that I go to do, but beyond that is to pass it on to someone else.

March 23 · Yes, it will get hard, but remember... if it's worth having its worth fighting for. Yes, you are going to want to give up, but remember if you give up you'll be back in the same place you were when you started. Yes, it is easy to quit, but those that maintain a relentless pursuit will achieve victory. Delay is not denial and if you focus you will eliminate fear. If you start...FINISH.

March 14 · Everything you need to get the job done is in your hand.

March 14 · Joseph had dreams of ruling, but was sold into slavery by his own brothers at 17. Spent 2 years in prison and became 2nd in command of Egypt at 30. It took at least 13 years to complete destiny, but what would've happened if he lost sight of the vision?

March 11 · At one point I thought numerology was random, but as I continued to dive into the Biblical significance of numbers you start to see that many things aren't that random at all. Not assuming the position of guru/theorist/crazy on anything, but I will say, pay attention. It's quite fascinating, actually.

March 10 · People love winners. That's who we like to work with. No one wants to partner with a loser. Remember that in all you go to do... Win and people will always want to be on your team.

March 9 · I wonder if any Americans have taken over Canada like the Canadians: Bieber, Drake and Celine, have done in the US?

March 9 · I'm tired of whack networking events. We must expect and demand more of people. I appreciate what others are doing, but I've recently learned a new classification system: buyer, seller or friend. If you aren't one of the 3, our interaction will be limited. Side Note: limiting the sellers.

March 7 · It's been so long since school, I forgot about Spring Break. There was once a time when we had calculated vacations.

March 1 · Consistency is the key to breakthrough. It's amazing what happens when you don't quit. I don't post this stuff just for you guys to read... Many times this is the outlet to remind my own self that I have to win.

March 1 · "Holy-wood" living life like the biggest celebrity I know, Jesus.

February 14 · Why is it that most of us have accepted lesser level thinking? You only accept what you allow.

February 14 · I'm not satisfied with just making it. The definition of average is the best of the worst and worst of the best. We were not created to be average. We should all survive and thrive!

February 12 · Life is an amazing journey. This past week has had to have been one of my best. Although I was always working towards something I found a mentor that was able to point me in the exact direction. Notice I didn't say right direction. Being accurate and being exact are two things that are similar but mean a world of difference.

February 10 · In life you need guidance. Since there is nothing new under the sun, find someone that's seen it and get them to tell you all about it.

February 9 · I don't purposefully practice isolation, but as you go higher there are fewer friends around you.

February 7 · I'm convinced that most advertisers & marketing people don't know when to move on to the next or at least switch it up. Know the pulse of your customers.

February 5 · Random Thought: I used to like VH1's Pop-up video and when they finally played a song I knew, I thought it was cool.

February 3 · You don't know how many minutes you are away from breakthrough...

February 2 · There is nothing like having friends that motivate you to better your best. Keep people that push you. To my homeboy in OR, thank you sir.

February 2 · Late night session. Nothing like an afterhours drive to clear your head.

January 31 · I'm on a mission… Has anyone seen an expensive car with a bumper sticker? I'm in search of a lambo with one that says "I love Jesus."

January 30 · There is nothing like getting paid for doing something you love. Even if you are not at that point, you can always take steps to get there.

January 29 · Favorite ol' school saying: kick rocks.

January 28 · I didn't become a cool kid until I became myself and not be those other idiots. Amazing what happens when you be who you are… Message!

January 27 · Don't be weary in well doing for you will reap, if you faint not. *In other words:* "Don't Quit!" Is it easy? No. Is it worth it? Absolutely!

January 26 ·The Word of the Day: Deduction. Normally means to reason or conclude, but today's reference is me not giving extra money to the government.

January 26 · I've said this multiple times, but get out of bondage to people! When you are really free and don't care, it's an unexplainable feeling.

January 26 · You can't be friends with everybody.

January 25 · Life can be so simple when you stop demeaning yourself to please other people.

January 25 · One of the most insightful lines I've recently heard: Real G's move in silence like in lasagna. That Lil' Wayne may just make it...

January 25 · If something is worth it, it requires an investment.

January 24 · There is a big difference between talking and having a voice.

January 24 · There are 2 games I hate to lose at: Monopoly and Air Hockey. Make that 4 games I hate to lose at: Monopoly, Air Hockey, Spades, & Phase 10.

January 22 · Physically climbed a mountain for the first time in my life. You guys gotta check it out. Surreal experience when you get to the top. And once you reach the top, it's all downhill from there...

January 20 · When you realize life is about the journey you really begin to enjoy the trip itself. Like the song says, "Live Like You Were Dying."

January 19 · Be on the lookout, my cell may change soon. Too accessible. I'm all for great ideas, but leave them on the office voicemail.

January 18 · If it don't excel, expel.

January 18 · I have made a commitment as a business and a brand to not do anything that is less than our best. Excellence is an art form and a standard.

January 18 · I'm in the position I am in because I think for myself while getting paid to think for others.

January 16 · I'm starting to believe there is no such thing as being underrated. If you want to take you career higher, brand better.

January 13 · Have you ever thought about how much of a front you put on for other people that really could care less about you?

January 8 · The coolest thing about growing up is knowing that you are smart enough to need help.

January 5 · If we're not living, why are we living?

January 5 · With me you got 1 minute, but I'll know in the first 30 seconds if the next 30 is even worth it.

January 5 · Being still and doing nothing are 2 different things.

January 4 · Now is the time to reinvent yourself. Don't worry... your "friends" will still be in the same place.

January 4 · Perfect conditions will never exist. Not saying be stupid, but if you're ready... go.

January 4 · You are who you think you are.

January 4 · If something is worth having, it's worth fighting for.

January 4 · The definition of average is the best of the worst and the worst of the best. Stand up and stand out.

January 3 · Life truly is a marathon and it's amazing what happens when you just stay in your assigned lane.

January 3 · I don't know if anyone else senses it, but breakthrough is on the horizon. The excitement is contagious and it ain't just new year jitters.

January 3 · Talent and Anointing are 2 different things.

January 3 · I've been broke, but I've never been poor. The former is temporary, the latter is a mindset. I ain't friends with either one of them now.

January 2 · Ever let someone borrow something, forget and then they loan you what you lent to them like it's theirs?

January 2 · Your Way or Yah-Weh?

January 2 · When value exceeds price, there is a sale every time. This relates to all facets of life, business, family, & relationships.

January 1 · Knowledge is power, but it takes wisdom to wield it.

January 1 · I wonder if Bible times were anything like today... Like the story with Solomon and the baby would be like Maury. #youareNOTthefather

January 1 · Life is not hard. Keep it simple and pay attention to your surroundings. Getting workout tips from a fat guy... #DoesntMakeSense

January 1 · New year, new you, new identity. Knew you then, know you now, I hope this change sticks.

8: TWO THOUSAND TEN
"The Year of The Reveal"

December 31 · "The ultimate reason for setting goals is to entice you to become the person it takes to achieve them." —Jim Rohn

December 28 · I started 2010 off with a dream. During the year my dream became reality. Unexpected? No. I mentally and physically mapped out all that was to take place. In saying this, I challenge you to dream again. Dream BIG, but don't stop with the dream. Act and pursue the things that you want in and out of life. A word of preparation- Don't Tell Everyone Your Dream! They'll Try to Kill It Just Because You Are Going Somewhere.

December 27 · "Winning isn't everything, it's the only thing." - V. Lombardi

December 23 · Ever have anyone negatively forecast your future? YOUR life is a result of the choices and decisions YOU make...

December 22 · It is my sincere hope that your past was but a sneak peek into the great things that are in store for your future.

December 22 · I'm determined to live a life of purpose. I know you may not understand this and that's cool, but at the end of the day, I don't answer to you.

December 19 · Question of the Day: If you only have 2 years left, what would you differently today?

December 14 · Self-reflection: Am I less than my best? If so, Why?

December 14 · It's amazing how much is accomplished when you take the time to listen first... then act.

December 12 · Questions in life: Why does the dough taste better than the cookie?

December 6 · Lessons in life: Don't fall for the set-up... Have you ever noticed how people bring you information just to see how you'll react or what you'll say? Real people that are productive and about business, have no time for foolishness. Keep it Movin'.

November 5 · In life you have opportunities, choices and destinations. The opportunity will present itself for you to make a choice and arrive at your destination. Always remember it was YOUR choice to end up where you are.

October 20 · Time + Maturity = Growth. I guess that's what people mean when they say, "live a little..."

July 29 · Don't quit. Don't ever quit. If it's worth fighting for, fight 'til the death. If they brought Lazarus back... Get ready for round 2.

April 28 · Getting closer and closer...

February 20 · I Got "NOW." I'll be next too...

February 17 · Sleep On It... "Success seems to be connected with action. Successful people keep moving. They make mistakes, but they don't quit."
– Conrad Hilton

January 6 · Are you busy or productive? "Acting" like you are accomplishing things will leave you upset when you realize you're still in the same place.

9: THE END OF THE BEGINNING

December 16, 2007 · You can't shake me. You won't break me... even after a 27-hour coma... People if you don't know that God is real... hit me up. I will testify and not testi'lie'.

P.S. > We just put an ending on a new beginning.

* **A Special Note:** If you have found this book to be informative, enlightening, humorous & engaging... Let me know! My various contact information has been provided in the 'About the Author' section and I look forward to learn of your experience. Also, please share your recommendation of this title with your colleagues, friends and social networks.

Thank You.
-Tony Rouse

Fun Fact: Did you notice that there is no printed text on the back cover of this book?!? I was inspired by billionaire hotelier, Steve Wynn, who when he created his namesake hotel Wynn Las Vegas, chose not put the 'show' on the outside of the venue like in his previous hotel ventures Bellagio and Treasure Island. So the reason this 'book has no back' is because I decided to house the information and adventure inside as opposed to presenting a full display merely for people passing by. In other words... Thank you for reading.

ABOUT THE AUTHOR

Tony Rouse is a Brand Strategy Specialist known as The Curator of High-End Experiences whose revolutionary concepts and projects have achieved international exposure and acclaim. He is a Myers-Briggs hybrid of "The Executive" (ENTJ) and "The Giver" (ENFJ) who created and defined the term, Fully Integrated Lifestyle Marketing (F.I.L.M.) which, as he sees it, takes an unconventional approach to traditional advertising by seamlessly creating experiences for brands in the lives of their target consumers and as such, has become the signature of his award-winning style. Having worked with over 25 Fortune 500 companies in the varied capacities of advisement, representation and consultation, he has also been an emcee on national tours for both NASCAR and Universal Records. By the age of 18, he was a featured performer at Carnegie Hall and today serves as a guest contributor for The Wall Street Business Network. Coupled with a healthy dose of witty wisdom and humorous understanding of the rapidly changing state of consumer affairs, taste, preferences and selection, he effortlessly relates to a world inundated with ever-evolving technology.

For More Information: www.MeetTonyRouse.com
Facebook/Instagram/Twitter: @MeetTonyRouse
Email: SayHello@MeetTonyRouse.com

Additional Titles by Tony Rouse:

Dare 2 D.R.E.A.M.:
The Basics of Building a Brand
(whether it be a person, product or project…)

Presentation Pep Talk:
The 20-Minute Quick Fix

Takeover Tuesday:
55 Short Stories to Help You
Win in Business & Life

www.ingramcontent.com/pod-product-compliance
Lightning Source LLC
Chambersburg PA
CBHW071638050426
42443CB00026B/722